Great
WINDOW
TREATMENTS

Great WINDOW TREATMENTS

Claire Martens

Sterling Publishing Co., Inc.
New York

A Sterling/Sewing Information Resources Book

Sewing Information Resources

Owner: JoAnn Pugh-Gannon
Photography: Brian Krause, Butterick Studio
Book Design and Electronic Page Layout: Ernie Shelton, Shelton Design Studios
Writer: Heidi King
Index: Anne Leach

Sewing Information Resources is a registered trademark of GANZ Inc.

A Sterling/Sewing Information Resources Book

1 3 5 7 9 10 8 6 4 2

First paperback edition published in 1998 by
Sterling Publishing Company, Inc.
387 Park Avenue South, New York, N.Y. 10016
Originally published in hardcover under the title
Clever Cornices, Valances & Unique Window Treatments
© 1997 by Sewing Information Resources
Distributed in Canada by Sterling Publishing
% Canadian Manda Group, One Atlantic Avenue, Suite 105
Toronto, Ontario, Canada M6K 3E7
Distributed in Great Britain and Europe by Cassell PLC
Wellington House, 125 Strand, London WC2R 0BB, England
Distributed in Australia by Capricorn Link (Australia) Pty Ltd.
P.O. Box 6651, Baulkham Hills, Business Centre, NSW 2153, Australia
Printed in China
All rights reserved

Sterling ISBN 0-8069-8647-6

Acknowledgments

ew books would exist today without the expert assistance of many people. It is these people and companies that we thank for all their efforts and hard work in making this such an exciting book project.

To the project designers for their unique, creative talents: Brent Pallas (cornices); Julia Bernstein (shutters); Sara Hochhauser (sewn valances); and Barri Seigal (flowers and frames).

To our suppliers for their generous contributions:

CM Offray & Son, Inc., Chester, NJ (ribbon)

VIP Fabric, New York, NY (fabric)

Artifact's, Inc., Palestine, TX (decoupage papers)

Diane Ericson, ReVisions®, Carmel, CA (Fall Leaves #3 stencil)

Quilters' Ranch, Inc., Tempe, AZ (Triangles on a Roll)

And a special thank you to the many "invisible" people — those behind the scenes that made this book happen.

Table of contents

Introduction

Every home is full of windows — large, small, or in-between, and of varying shapes or styles. If you possess a fantastic view of the mountains or of the sea, you may want to leave your windows completely alone and enjoy the view! But often, your windows need a finishing touch to complete the decoration of your room.

Explore the projects outlined throughout this book and find the one that's perfect for your situation. Or use these ideas as a starting point to stimulate your own creativity — employ a sense of humor, a lightness of touch, a burst of color, or create a uniqueness with your window treatments not found elsewhere. Don't be afraid to test and experiment with styles and designs before settling on the "right" treatment for your windows. We have attempted to give you many unique and different ideas, all very easy to make on your own.

Combine the ideas, like using the Adirondack Style cornice (page 40) with the Rustic Twigs shutters (page 108) to finish that den or getaway cottage. Or match the designs on the Victorian Decoupage cornice (page 122) and the Decorative Decoupage shutters (page 96) to create an inviting and elegant dining room. Add sheer curtains, discreet blinds, or cafe curtains to any one of the ideas given here for additional privacy.

But remember, have fun!

CHAPTER 1

Working With Your Window

The right window dressing can completely transform the look and feel of a room. To help you make a thoughtful, well-informed decision, educate yourself about the various styles, fabrics, sewing techniques, and installation procedures associated with the window treatment of your choice.

From simple-stitched valances to sophisticated cornice boards, it is surprisingly easy and inexpensive to make your own window treatments.

Perhaps no other decorating element changes the appearance of a room more drastically than a window treatment. Whereas a bare window blends inconspicuously into the background, a well-dressed window flaunts its features and often becomes the focal point of a room.

Centuries ago, windows were merely small holes punched through walls so that smoke and fumes could escape from inside. Later, they evolved into larger openings, often left bare to make the most of available natural light. Shutters were added when privacy became a concern.

The first curtains were strictly utilitarian, consisting of nothing more than a piece of fabric attached above the window or over rough walls to protect against cold and drafts. It wasn't until the nineteenth century that windows began to be draped and decorated with lavish fabrics and trims.

Today, window treatments still provide privacy and insulation, but they are most valued for their decorative aspects. By combining color, texture, design, and style, window treatments add an exciting and innovative dimension to an overall decorating scheme.

This book offers an artful approach to decorating windows. By following the inspirational photographs, helpful diagrams, and user-friendly instructions, you will not only learn how to emphasize a window's architectural features, but also how to transform windows with no distinct character of their own into masterful displays.

Choosing the Correct Window Treatment

Dressing windows can be a considerable investment of both time and money. To help you make an informed decision, ask yourself the following questions before choosing a window treatment.

Does the window treatment enhance the positive features of the window and de-emphasize its flaws? For example, a window with unusual architectural molding or stained glass needs only a simple valance or cornice to transform it into the focal point of a room. Likewise, decorative shutters or blinds will disguise uneven wood trim and add interest to ordinary windowpanes.

How many windows must be covered?

Selecting treatments for a room with several windows of different shapes and sizes can be challenging. For a unifying look, choose one fabric and treatment for all windows. Consider windows such as bay windows and horizontal windows that are installed close together as a single unit. Finally, keep in mind that simple designs for window treatments generally create a more cohesive look.

Will the window be functional? If the window will be used for air circulation, select shutters, a pretty valance, or any other type of window treatment that will not interfere with opening and closing the window.

Is privacy a concern? If so, the window treatment should cover the entire window. Shutters and blinds are obvious choices, but you also can install retractable blinds behind a cornice or valance that pull up and out of sight during the day.

How much natural warmth and light do you want in the room? Attractive toppers accentuate the window and permit the maximum amount of light to flood into the room. Shutters and blinds allow you to control the amount of light. When closed, they also act as insulators against the cold during the winter and block the heat from sunlight during the summer.

What is the decorative style of the room? The style of the room should influence the style of the window treatment you choose. If the windows are to be the focal point, choose bold colors and striking treatments that demand attention upon entering the room. If the windows act as a backdrop to the furnishings, choose subtle treatments in matching fabrics. For an authentic, period look, research the particular era and then make your decision accordingly.

Fabric Basics

The choice of fabrics has never been greater, creating an array of decorating possibilities. But narrowing to one fabric scheme can be overwhelming. Begin by examining the basics of fabric: color, tex-

ture, pattern, weight, and weave.

Color, or lack of it, is the most noticeable aspect of fabric. Bold, dark colors absorb and minimize the amount of light that shines through the window. They also add drama to a neutral background and turn the window into the focal point of the room. Light colors maintain the amount of light coming through the window and give the illusion of added brightness. Certain colors can visually enlarge the window or enclose it.

Texture adds depth and dimension to fabric. Its tactile qualities contribute to the atmosphere and style of a room and create a link between contrasting fabric colors. Many textures absorb sound and possess reflective light qualities that make a room seem larger. Shiny textures like satin and taffeta reflect light and brighten the surface of the fabrics. Rough textures such as burlap and tweed reduce the impact of bright light, which produces a calm, relaxed look. Light-filtering textures such as lace and voile diffuse light, creating a soft, soothing effect in a room.

Pattern enriches the overall look of fabrics. Besides adding rhythm, movement, depth, and imagery, a specific pattern can coordinate several otherwise mismatched pieces of fabric into a cohesive scheme. When selecting a pattern, look for balance in both scale and proportion. Large patterns will dominate a room and create a busy and stimulating space. They are ideal for spacious areas, since they make the room seem less intimidating and more cozy and inviting; in small rooms, they overpower, closing in the walls, ceiling, and floor. Small patterns appear to recede and can fade into the background if the color scheme is bland. They work best in small areas by producing the illusion of space.

The **weight** and **weave** of fabric determines how it will drape when hanging in the window. Lightweight, loosely woven fabrics such as linen and gingham have an open, airy appearance and are good choices when a tailored look is desired. However, they also have a tendency to shrink and sag with changes in temperature and humidity. Damask, canvas, and other heavy, densely woven fabrics work well for treatments that will be routinely opened and closed. Because of their tight weave, dense fabrics block light and are ideal to use when total privacy is desired.

Selecting Fabrics

When coupled with the appropriate style, any type of fabric can be used effectively to make a window treatment. In fact, some of the most exciting combinations are daring and unconventional. For example, lightweight towels, bed linens, and even cloth shower curtains can be stitched into stunning valances and blinds for the window. Yet how do you know if you will be able to live indefinitely with a certain fabric and window treatment?

Your best bet is to keep the basic aspects of fabric in mind, but then allow your personal preferences to dictate your choices. These tips will help you identify your perennial fabric favorites.

■ Begin by assembling your favorite fabric swatches, magazine pictures of window treatments, and photographs of furniture and accessories from the room you are decorating and carry them with you to the fabric store.

■ Choose several fabrics you like, lay them on a flat surface, and compare them with the swatches and pictures.

■ Weed out fabrics that do not match the furniture and accessories you plan to use.

■ Look for similarities between the fabric and your favorite fabric swatches.

■ Imagine the fabrics being used in the various pictures you've selected of window treatments. When you've narrowed your selection to three or four, ask for fabric swatches.

At home, tape the fabric swatches to the window frame or pin them to existing drapes. After several days, you will begin to notice subtleties, such as which fabrics catch your eye upon entering the room, which fabrics seem to fade into the background, and which fabrics coordinate easily with your furnishings.

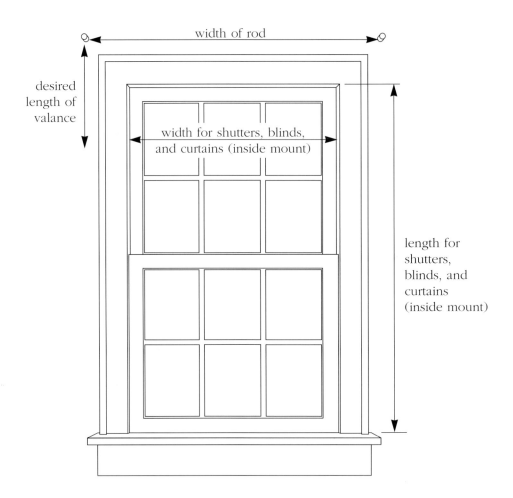

width of rod

desired length of valance

width for shutters, blinds, and curtains (inside mount)

length for shutters, blinds, and curtains (inside mount)

Measuring Your Window

Correct measurements are essential to creating a window treatment that fits your window perfectly. For accuracy, use a metal measuring stick instead of a fabric tape measure, and measure each window, since they can be slightly different in size.

Before measuring, install the hardware for the window treatment, if any, to help you visualize the finished look. Generally, curtain rods are placed 2 to 4 inches above the top of the window frame, or if inside the window, 1 inch below the top of the frame. Make sure the hardware is level, even if the window itself, is not.

For curtains and valances, measure vertically from the hardware to the desired length, and horizontally the width of the curtain rod.

For shutters, blinds, and curtains that are installed inside the window frame, measure the length of the window from the inside top to the inside bottom of the frame; for the width, measure horizontally inside the window frame.

16

LENGTH SPECIFICATIONS

MEASUREMENT
(in inches)

A. **Finished Length** measure vertically from bottom of curtain rod to desired length	
B. **Hem Allowance** simple curtains and valances: add at least 4"	
C. **Casings (rod pockets)** add diameter of rod plus 1" for ease *add 2" for heavy, densely woven fabrics	
D. **Heading** (decorative ruffle above curtain rod) add twice the desired height of the heading	
E. **TOTAL SUM OF LENGTH SPECIFICATIONS**	

WIDTH SPECIFICATIONS

MEASUREMENT
(in inches)

F. **Finished Width** measure width of window or curtain rod	
G. **Fullness** multiply window width by 3 *for heavy, densely woven fabrics, multiply window width by 2	
H. **Seam Allowance** simple curtains and valances: add 1" for each side seam	
I. **TOTAL SUM OF WIDTH SPECIFICATIONS**	
J. **Number of Panels Desired**	
K. **Panel Width** divide total width (I) by number of desired panels (J)	

DETERMINING YARDAGE

MEASUREMENT
(in inches)

L. **Panel Measurement** multiply total length (E) by number of panels desired (J) *for example, 3 panels at 10" in length require 30" in fabric	
M. **Convert Inches to Yards** divide total number of inches (L) by 36 " *for example, 110" ÷ 36"	

EXTRA YARDAGE FOR PATTERNED FABRICS	MEASUREMENT (in inches)
A. **Design Repeat** measure the length of one design or pattern in the fabric	
B. **Amount Needed for Each Panel** multiply the design repeat (A) by the number of panels needed	
C. **Convert Inches to Yards** divide total number of inches (B) by 36" *for example, 110" ÷ 36"	
D. **TOTAL AMOUNT OF EXTRA YARDAGE NEEDED**	

Determining Yardage for Patterned Fabrics

Extra yardage is needed when working with patterned fabrics because the repeated designs must be matched. In general, the larger the pattern, the longer the design repeat will be, and the more waste fabric you will have.

Before cutting, decide where you want the design to fall on the window treatment. For a full-length curtain, a design at eye level or just above is easier to see than a design positioned along the hem. The opposite is true for a valance, where the hem is the most visible. Each panel for each window should be cut so the design falls in the same exact position.

If you must piece fabric together horizontally to create panels, be sure to align the patterns in the fabric. Unmatched patterns are extremely noticeable and detract from the effectiveness of your window treatment.

The easiest way to figure extra yardage is to add the length of one pattern or design repeat to the length of every panel. This, however, can produce

unnecessary waste fabrics. For a more accurate measurement, use the chart above to determine how much extra fabric you will need for pattern repeats.

Preparing the Fabric

Unlike garment fabric, decorator fabrics used for window treatments do not require prewashing and preshrinking. In fact, washing the fabrics can remove their body, crispness, and shine. If you must clean the fabric, have it dry-cleaned or hang it outside to air. Once the window treatment is made, you can use the brush attachment on your vacuum cleaner to remove lint and dust.

If the fabric is creased, iron it on a low temperature setting on the wrong side of the fabric.

When the fabric is ready to cut, lay it on a flat surface and position it so the curtain is cut along the lengthwise and crosswise grain. To find the grain in the fabric, pull one or two threads from selvage to selvage and cut on the resulting line. You also can use a carpenter's square or quilting ruler to create a line that is perpendicular to the selvage. For fabric with a printed design, use the design as a guide for cutting. If the design seems crooked, it is best to choose another type of fabric.

Piecing Fabrics

Piecing fabrics together may be required to create panels in the desired width. For panels with an even number of pieces, simply stitch the pieces together. For odd-numbered pieces, stitch the middle pieces of the panel together. Cut the last piece in half lengthwise and then stitch one half to each end of the panel so the design is continuous.

Setting Up Your Sewing Machine and Serger

Proper machine setup is essential for even stitches and a smooth, professional finish.

Thread. Choose a thread that matches or is slightly darker than the fabric. Polyester or polyester/cotton blends produce the best results. This thread tends to stretch, so if the seam line seems to pucker during sewing, loosen the upper tension on your machine. An alternative is to use monofilament or clear thread for stitching, which eliminates match-ing the color. Take care when pressing seams stitched with these threads, as they are heat sensitive.

Needles. Most fabrics require a size 80/14 needle. For heavy, stiff fabrics, use a size 90/16 needle. Change your needle frequently. If you hear a punching sound as the needle moves down through the fabric, your needle is dull and should be changed.

Presser Feet. Most window treatments can be stitched with a regular or all-purpose presser foot. Some machines have specialized feet which makes sewing faster and easier, and improves the quality of your work. There are several types of presser feet which might be beneficial.

■ *A zipper foot* is used to make and insert piping. There are also more specialized cording or piping feet that produce a professional finish.

■ *A walking or even-feed foot* has an additional feeding system on top of the fabric to assist the feed dogs in feeding multiple layers of fabric together. This is especially helpful for napped fabrics like velvet or corduroy. It also can help in matching plaids and other pattern motifs.

■ *Hemmers* turn the fabric under twice and hem it at the same time. Available in a number of sizes, they can accommodate different weights of fabrics

and stitch hems in different widths.

■ A *ruffler or gathering foot* gathers fabric for ruffles or frills. It can gather one fabric and stitch it to an ungathered piece of fabric at the same time.

■ A *blindhem foot* creates a blindhem stitch on the sewing machine. This type of hem is less visible and has a hand-stitched appearance.

■ A *binder foot* folds over and attaches decorative bindings or edgings to fabric at one time.

Serger Feet

■ A *blindhem foot* allows you to cut off the edge of the fabric, finish the hem edge, and hem the fabric all at once. It has a commercial finish.

■ A *piping or multi-purpose foot* makes piping, while stitching it to a flat piece of fabric. It produces a professional finish in very little time.

■ A *binder* for a serger performs the same function as a sewing machine binder, but in less time.

Standard Machine Settings

Sewing Machine. A stitch length of **2-3,** or 10 to 12 stitches per inch, is adequate for stitching both running and zigzag stitches. If the stitch length is too short, it can cut into and even tear the fabric. Some fabrics retain needle holes, so alter the stitch length accordingly to prevent this.

Serger. Because a wide, stable seam is needed, set the serger for a four-thread, balanced overlock stitch. Use polyester or polyester/cotton blend thread in the needles and matching serger thread in the loopers. The stitch length should be **2-2.5,** with a suitable cutting width of slightly less than **2.** Use a neutral setting for the differential feed. You also can set the differential feed from **1-2** to help match designs and keep the panel lengths even, and a **.5-.8** setting to eliminate puckering.

stitching Tips

Simple seams are all that is required to make any of the window treatments featured in this book. To keep the seams straight during stitching, hold the fabric taut without stretching it, and be sure to support the fabric in front of and behind the needle. Because the seams must be durable, secure the beginning and ending of a seam line with a few backstitches.

While a flat seam can be used for most window treatments, there are several different seams that work best for certain types of fabrics and functions.

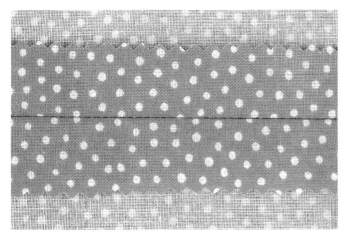

A *plain flat seam* is the basic seam type and is made with a simple running stitch. To make a plain flat seam, pin the fabric pieces together with right sides facing and raw edges aligned, then stitch the fabric pieces together with a $1/2$- to 1-inch seam allowance. Press the seam open using a pressing cloth between the iron and fabric. If the selvage has not been trimmed from the edges of the fabric, it should be clipped every three inches to keep the flat seam from becoming uneven. If the selvage is cut off, another seam type must be used.

A *French seam* is a seam within a seam. It is most often used on sheer or lightweight fabrics that fray easily or to cover raw edges of the fabric that might be visible. To make a French seam, pin the *wrong* sides of the fabric together and stitch in place. Trim the seam allowance to $1/8$ inch. Press the seam open, then fold along the seam line so the right sides of the fabric are facing. Press and baste in place. To finish, stitch $1/4$ inch from the first seam line, or close enough to enclose the first seam. Press the seam to one side.

A **_flat fell seam_** is a durable seam that creates a neat, professional finish on both sides of the fabric. It is ideal for enclosing raw edges on mid- to heavy-

weight fabrics. You can stitch the seam on either side of the fabric you choose. Begin with the _wrong_ sides of the fabric together; pin and stitch along the seam line. Press the seam open, then press both seam allowances to one side. Trim the seam underneath to half its width. Turn the upper seam over the trimmed seam and pin in place. Topstitch along the turned-over edge, then press flat. You also can use a feller foot to create this seam.

A **_serger seam_** stitches the seam, trims the seam allowance, and finishes the raw edge all at once. To reinforce loosely woven fabrics, first stitch the seam on a sewing machine, then restitch with a serger.

Stitching Patterned Fabrics

There are three methods to use when fabrics have designs that must be matched. Be sure to press the seams thoroughly after each stitching.

■ Match the pattern designs, then pin the fabric pieces together with right sides facing. Use a walking or even-feed foot while stitching to keep the fabric layers from shifting. Remove the pins as you approach them on the machine.

■ Match the designs at the selvages. On most decorator fabrics, only half of the design falls at the selvage. To match patterns from the right side of the fabric, turn one edge of the fabric under along the selvage and pin in place over the other piece to be joined. Make sure patterns are aligned. Stitch close to the fold on the right side of the fabric, then stitch another parallel seam ¼ inch away from the first.

■ Use fusible web tape to align the designs. Press under one selvage or seam allowance. Iron the fusible web on the top of the other selvage. Overlap the two and press in place. Topstitch to secure.

The Perfect Hem

The best hems are never noticed, because they blend inconspicuously with the fabric. For a smooth, flawless hem, turn the bottom edge of the fabric under at least 2 inches to the wrong side and press. You can vary the width of the hem as desired, using the length of the valance or curtain as a guide. Turn the fabric under again and pin in place; press flat. To finish the hem, choose one of these four options:

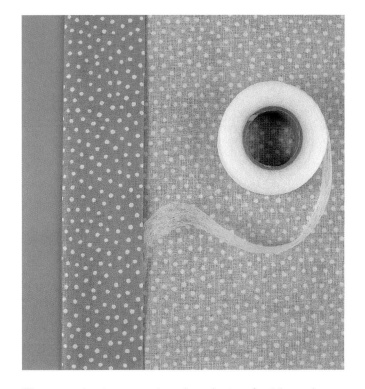

■ ***Fuse the hem*** in place by placing fusible web tape between the folds of the hem. Be sure to pretest the fabric to determine whether it can withstand the high temperature and moisture necessary to melt the webbing.

■ Use a ***sewing machine blindhem stitch*** to complete the window treatment. Fold the pressed hem to the right side of the fabric, offsetting the edge of

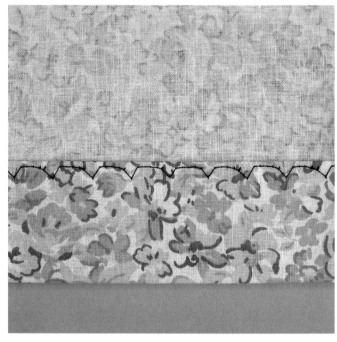

■ Stitch the hem with a ***basic running stitch.*** Set the stitch at **3**, or eight to 10 stitches per inch, so that it is slightly longer than the normal stitch length.

the hem so the bottom ⅛ inch of the hem falls on the wrong side of the fabric. Using the blindhem stitch setting, guide the edge of the hem through the machine. The straight-stitch portion of the blindhem stitch should fall on the actual edge of the hem and the zigzag portion should grab the fold on the main part of the fabric. Adjust the setting as needed to create a stitch that barely shows on the right side of the window treatment. If desired, use monofilament thread to completely hide the stitching.

■ Finish the hem with a *serger blindhem stitch.* When using the serger, fold the total hem allowance up only once, offsetting the edge of the hem ¼ to ½ inch. Thread the serger needle with monofilament thread. The machine will serge, cut, finish the raw edge, and hem the window treatment at the same

Casings

time. For a flatter hem, set the serger for a flatlock stitch. If you use a blindhem serger foot, adjust the foot so the needle falls along the fold.

Finishing the Side Edges

Side hems can be finished in the same manner as bottom hems. The only difference is the side edges are turned under ½ inch twice, instead of 2 inches or more. Once the hems are stitched and pressed, tack small curtain weights to the inside of the lower side hems to help the curtains hang straight. For heavy fabrics, slide heavy chains into the bottom hem before finishing the side hems.

A **casing,** or rod pocket, is a wide hem along the top edge of the window treatment which conceals the curtain rod. A simple casing is created in the same manner as the bottom hem. To determine the depth of the casing, measure the diameter of the curtain rod and add one inch for ease. Add 2 inches for heavier fabrics. Finish the casing by turning the raw edge under ½ inch and stitching with a straight stitch. If desired, topstitch near the top folded edge of the window treatment.

Headings

To **create a heading**, or decorative ruffle, along the top of the window treatment, fold the top edge under ¼ inch twice and stitch in place. Press flat. Fold the stitched edge under the desired width of the heading, plus the desired width of the casing, then stitch in place. Press flat. Measure and mark the placement line for the top of the casing and bottom of the heading, then stitch along the placement line to finish.

Creating Ruffles

Simple ruffles add fullness and style to the edges of window treatments. For best results, select light-weight fabrics, since they lie flatter than heavy fabrics and are easier to gather.

To determine the length needed for a ruffle, measure the edge of the window treatment where the ruffle will be attached and multiply by 2½. For sheer fabrics, multiply by 3.

To determine the width of the ruffle, cut a strip of fabric the desired width, plus 1 inch for seam allowances. Fold one long edge under ¼ inch twice and stitch in place. For a double ruffle, cut a strip of fabric twice the desired width, plus ¼ inch, then fold so the wrong sides are facing. No hemming is necessary.

When the ruffle has been cut and the raw edges finished, complete the ruffle with one of the simple gathering techniques.

Gathering

Gathering is a basic way to draw up fabric along a stitching line. There are five basic ways to gather ruffles:

■ **Gathering stitch.** This technique works best for lightweight fabrics. Set the machine at the longest stitch length possible. Topstitch two or three parallel rows along the top of the ruffle, just outside the seam line. Leave long thread tails at each end. Gently pull the threads from both ends to create the desired amount of gathers. Pin the gathered fabric to the ungathered fabric so the gathers are evenly distributed. Stitch in place, then remove the visible gathering threads.

■ **Cording gathers.** Pin a strong piece of cord, string, or yarn in place along the top of the ruffle. Set the sewing machine to a stitch length and zigzag width of **2.** Beginning at one end, stitch the cord to the ruffle, adjusting the zigzag as needed so the cord is not caught in the stitching. Pull the cording to create the gathers. This method is ideal for double ruffles and for full ruffles stitched from medium- to heavyweight fabrics.

■ **Ruffler.** A ruffler is suitable for single and double ruffles in all fabric weights. Additionally, it can be used to pleat fabric, which produces a tailored

■ *Gathering foot.* This useful sewing machine foot is used to gather both single or double ruffles. Long stitch lengths, tight tension settings, and lightweight fabrics will create the fullest gathers. For best results, stitch ½ inch from the edge of the fabric. When gathering a double ruffle, baste the two layers together before stitching. This foot also allows you to gather the ruffle and stitch it to an ungathered piece of fabric. Consult your sewing machine manual for specific instructions.

finish. By adjusting the ruffler settings, you can change the number of stitches between rufflers or pleats, and the amount of fabric used for each. A ruffler also can ruffle fabric and stitch it to an ungathered piece of fabric or between two pieces of fabric at the same time. If desired, ribbon or other narrow trims can be added to the window treatment while ruffling or pleating.

Shirring Tapes

Shirring tape is a strip of fabric that features several rows of pre-stitched cording, thus eliminating the need for machine gathering. Depending on the style you choose, you can create a smocked heading, or

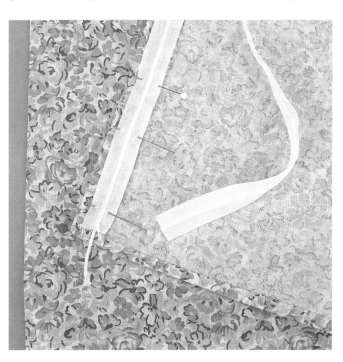

■ **Serger gathering.** Using the longest stitch length and maximum differential feed possible, a serger turns lightweight fabric into ruffles. With the help of an attachment, the fabric can be ruffled and serged to an ungathered piece of fabric at the same time. It is also possible to gather by serging a four-thread balanced overlock stitch at a stitch length of **3** and then gently pulling on the needle threads only. These methods work best for lightweight fabric.

traditional, box, or pencil pleats. Fusible shirring tape is extremely quick to use, but works best with unlined window treatments made from lightweight fabrics. Traditional shirring tape is stitched to the fabric and can be used for both lined and unlined window treatments.

To use the shirring tape to gather a window treatment, cut and hem the curtain or valance along the bottom and side edges. Cut a piece of shirring tape the same width as the top edge of the valance, plus two inches. If needed, stitch a casing for the curtain rod, and if desired, a decorative heading along the top of the valance. Pin the tape in place along the stitching line. Using a seam ripper, remove one inch from each row of cording at each end of the tape, then turn the ends of the tape under and pin in place. Stitch or fuse the tape in place. Tie the ends of the cording together at one end of the tape, then pull the cords on the other end to gather the fabric. When gathers have been adjusted to the desired length, tie the ends of the cords together and trim.

piping

Traditional piping adds a decorative accent to the seams of a window treatment. You can purchase pre-stitched piping in a variety of colors and thicknesses, or you can make your own by covering cording with decorative fabric. Because the seam allowances of piping are stitched in-between the seams of the window treatment, it is best to use a lightweight fabric to cover the cording.

Begin by cutting widths of fabric the circumference of the cording, plus the width of two seam allowances. Traditionally, the fabric is cut on the bias, but if there are few curves in your project, you can cut it along the straight grain of the fabric. Join the fabric pieces as needed to create one continuous strip of fabric. Fold the long edges of the fabric together and press, then wrap it around the cording so raw edges are aligned. Using a zipper foot, stitch the fabric together as close as possible to the cording. Clip up to the seam allowance so the piping will lay flat.

To stitch **cording into a seam**, sandwich the piping between both pieces of fabric so the right sides are facing and raw edges are aligned; pin in place. Machine-stitch along the original seam line of the piping.

Shirred piping offers a soft, romantic look. A large diameter cord is used and the fabric is cut with additional width for gathering ease.

To make shirred piping, cut piping the desired length, then measure and cut fabric at least twice the length of the cording. Fold the long edges of the fabric together and press, then fold the fabric over

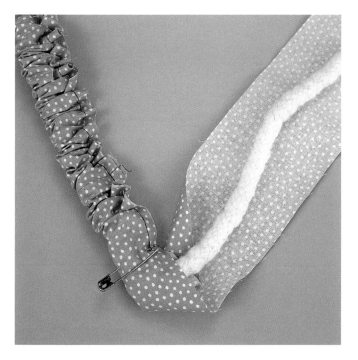 

the cording and stitch in place at one end. Using a zipper foot, stitch 10 inches along the edge of the cording. With the needle down into the fabric, raise the zipper foot and pull the cording forward to create gathers in the fabric. Continue stitching and gathering until the cording is completely covered with gathered fabric. Secure by stitching the fabric to the cording across the remaining end. Adjust gathers as desired.

Serger piping simplifies the process of making piping. Most sergers have a specialized foot designed to feed finished piping under the presser foot, and some even have a guide that holds the fabric in position while wrapping the cording. Because serger piping has a finished edge, it is ideal to use when there are several layers of fabric stitched together in one seam, or when an unusual fabric has been used to make the piping.

Cornice Basics

The cornices featured in this book frame the top and sides of a window. They consist of two end boards on the sides, a facing that covers the front of the window, and a narrow dust board that covers the top of the cornice.

To make a basic cornice board, begin by measuring your window. Install any hardware such as curtains or blinds first, then measure horizontally from the outside edges of the hardware and add 2 inches, or from the outside edges of the window frame, adding 1 inch to the measurement.

For best results, choose a 1 inch-thick, smooth wood with few knotholes such as pine to make your cornice board. To eliminate the steps for cutting the boards, take your measurements with you to the building supply and have them cut the boards to size.

constructing a cornice

For the facing, cut a 1"x6" board to the desired horizontal measurement. Cut two end boards from 1"x4" wood the same vertical measurement as the facing. For the dust board, cut a 1"x4" board the same width as the facing.

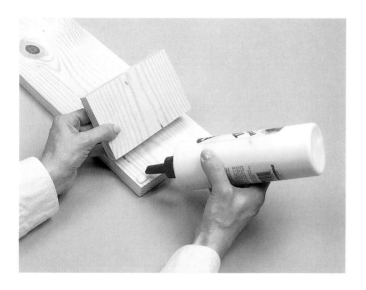

To assemble the cornice, apply wood glue along the side edges of the facing. Position one end board on each side of facing so front edges are aligned; nail in place with 1" finishing nails.

Slide dust board between end boards and align with top edge of facing; nail in place with 1" finishing nails. Wipe away excess wood glue from all joints. If desired, countersink nails, filling in holes with wood filler.

When the glue is dry, sand the cornice with medium-grade sandpaper and wipe clean with a damp cloth. For additional support, install two L-brackets along each inside corner of the cornice board, one at the top of the corner and the other at the bottom.

Mounting the cornice

Once the cornice has been embellished, position it at the top of the window so the sides are flush with the outside of the window frame. Using wood screws and L-brackets, attach the cornice to the window frame.

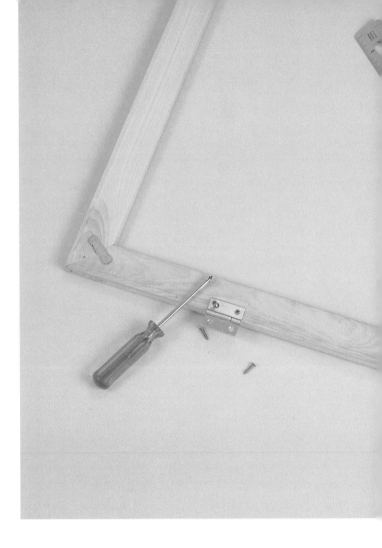

Constructing a Simple Shutter Frame

One of the easiest ways to make a shutter is to assemble artist's stretcher strips to fit the size of the window. Begin by measuring the length and width of the inside of the window frame; divide by 2. For each shutter, purchase two stretcher strips the length of the window and two strips one-half the width of the window, minus twice the width of the stretcher strip. Assemble the strips according to manufacturers instructions.

Another simple way to make a shutter frame is to fasten strips of lattice together with corrugated or crimped wood fasteners. For each shutter, cut two lattice strips the length of the window and two strips one-half the width of the window, minus twice the width of the lattice strip. Position the strips on a flat surface, butting side edge of top and bottom strips against side strips. All outside edges of frame should be parallel. Fasten the strips together with corrugated wood fasteners.

Mounting a Shutter

Purchase two hinges for each shutter. Position hinges on back of shutter along outside edge and screw in place. One should be positioned at the top of the shutter and the other at the bottom. Position shutter in window and mark placement for hinges along inside of window frame. To mount shutter, screw hinges to window frame.

Enlarging and Transferring Patterns

The easiest way to enlarge patterns and templates is to use a photocopier, adjusting the percentage as needed until the templates fit across the cornice facing. Be sure to leave at least 1-inch space along the cornice, above and below the templates.

To transfer the templates, trace the outlines onto tracing paper. You then can cut out the templates or position the tracing paper over carbon paper and trace the outline directly onto the wood.

CHAPTER 2

clever cornices

ornices do more than cover installation hardware — they add a crowning finish to your window. Made from three pieces of wood and mounted on the outside of the window frame, a cornice can be covered with fabric, painted with colorful motifs, or embellished with household odds and ends.

Child's Room
School Days

Inspired by old-fashioned schoolhouse motifs, a blackboard cornice is a smart way to decorate a child's window. For a personalized alternative, center and paint the child's name on the cornice instead of the ABC's.

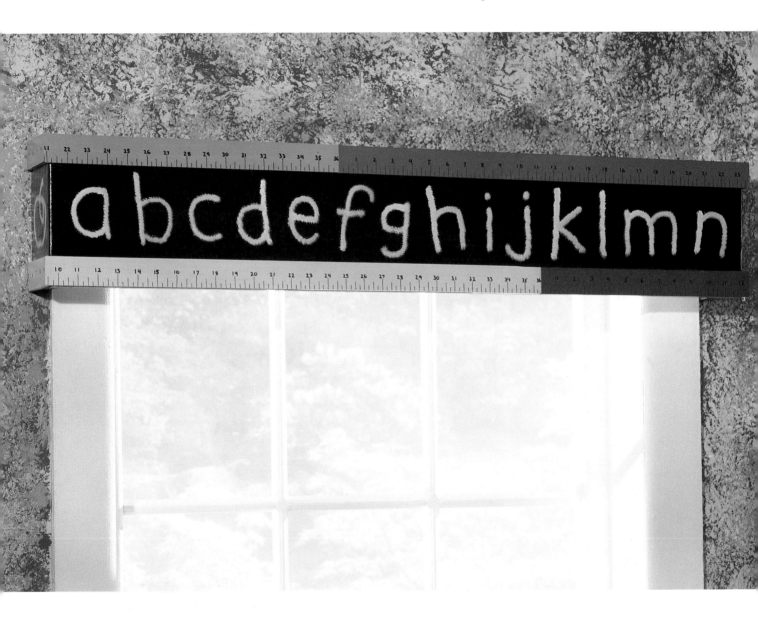

1

Sand cornice smooth and wipe with damp cloth. Using sponge brush, paint all sides of cornice with black paint. Apply additional coats of paint as needed until cornice is deep black. Let dry.

2

Cut two lattice strips same length as facing, plus ½", and four strips same length as end boards. Paint strips and let dry. Add lines with fine marker and numbers with extra fine marker.

3

If desired, miter corners of strips, then position along cornice top and bottom, aligning edges; nail in place with ½" brads. To avoid mitering, overlap facing strips over side strips. Paint over nails.

4

Draw lowercase letters along cornice front, spacing evenly between each. Using dry stencil brush, lightly dab white paint along outlines to create chalk-like letters. Let dry, then varnish.

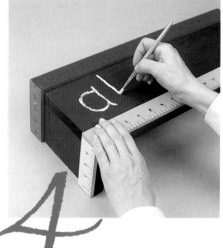

MATERIALS

Pre-assembled cornice (*Ch. 1*)
Sandpaper & damp cloth
Sponge brush

Assorted acrylic paints
¼"x 1⅜" lattice strips
Fine & extra fine black markers

Miter box (optional)
½"-diameter brads & hammer
¼"-diameter stencil brush
Clear, non-yellowing varnish

Den
Adirondack Style

Reflect the rustic character of a country interior by covering an ordinary cornice board with handmade bark paper. To finish the look, embellish the cornice with simple, geometric designs fashioned from straight, thin twigs.

1 Mix one part glue with eight parts water. Apply several coats of glue mixture to paper and wood on cornice with sponge brush; let dry. Fold paper over all edges of cornice; staple in place with staple gun.

2 Once paper is fastened securely, nail twigs around facing edges with 1" paneling nails. To determine geometric design, position string as desired on facing and secure in place with thumb tacks.

3 Cut and piece twigs as needed to create geometric design. Position twigs over string and nail in place, removing string and thumb tacks as you go. Center nails to avoid splitting twigs.

MATERIALS

Clear drying craft glue

Water

Handmade paper

Pre-assembled cornice *(Ch. 1)*

Sponge brush

Staple gun and staples

Twigs, about ¼" diameter

1" paneling nails

String

Thumb tacks

Kitchen
A Bevy of Birdhouses

Evoke the handcrafted charm of country style with a whimsical birdhouse cornice. Before cutting the two-story birdhouse, measure from the bottom edge of the cornice to your ceiling to be sure the birdhouse will fit.

Enlarge template to width of facing. Transfer to 1"x 12" piece of wood and cut out with coping saw. Nail wood to facing. Referring to photo and using rooflines as a guide, mark birdhouse sections.

Tape edges of alternate birdhouses, then paint with two coats of paint. Let dry. Remove tape and repeat for remaining birdhouses. For a distressed finish, lightly sand painted surface.

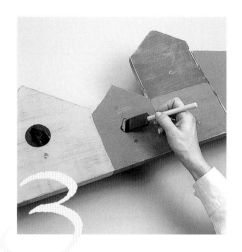

Center and draw ³/₄"- diameter circles on two-story birdhouse and 1¹/₂"- diameter circles on remaining houses; paint black. With drill and ³/₈"- diameter bit, drill hole underneath each circle.

Using coping saw, cut dowel into 2"- long pieces. Fill hole on each birdhouse with wood glue, then insert dowels so ends are aligned with back side of cornice. Wipe away excess glue and let dry.

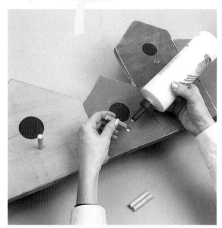

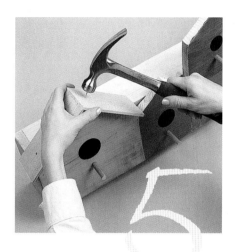

Beginning on left side, cut lattice strips for roof of first birdhouse, overlapping as needed to fit. Align back edges so strips create overhang along front, then nail in place. Repeat for all birdhouses.

MATERIALS

Pre-assembled cornice *(Ch. 1)*

1"x 12" piece of wood

Coping saw

Finishing nails

Masking tape

Acrylic paints & sponge brush

Coarse grade sandpaper

Drill & ³/₈"-diameter drill bit

³/₈"-diameter dowel

Wood glue & damp cloth

¹/₄"x 3¹/₂" lattice strips

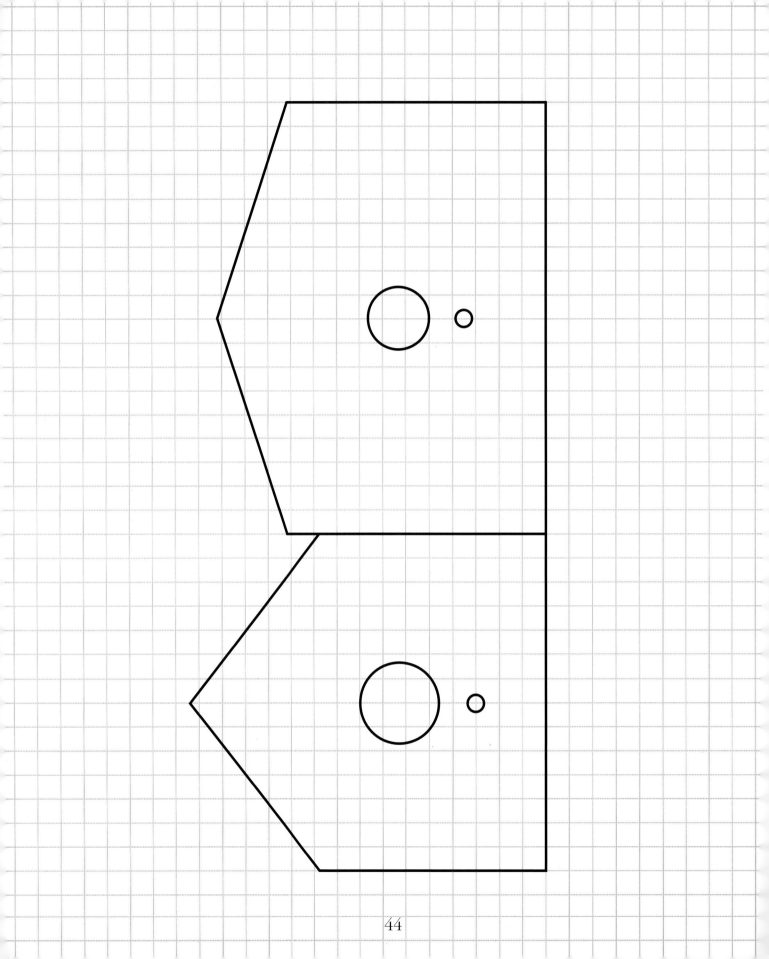

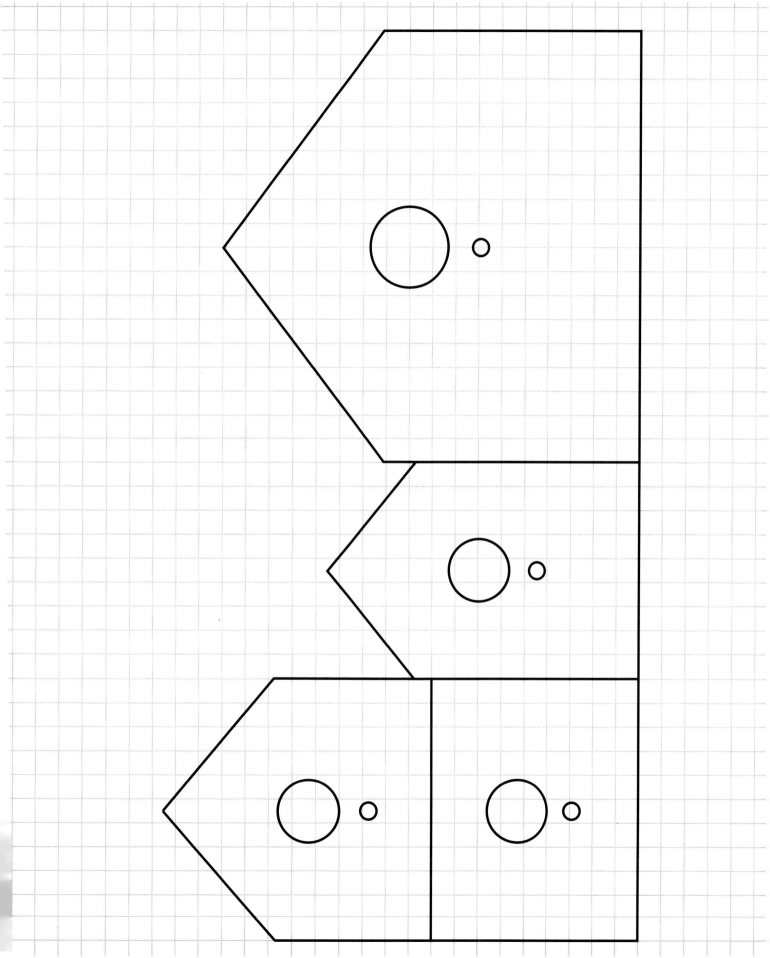

Child's Room
Noah's Ark

Lighthearted and soft, this painted cornice makes a proper topper for a nursery or young child's room. Use colors from bed linens and walls as inspiration, or create a lively scene by substituting primary paints for the pastel colors.

Enlarge templates to fit across facing, then transfer to tracing paper. Using sponge brush, paint cornice with several coats of white paint; let dry. Paint 2" light green stripe along bottom edges of all sides.

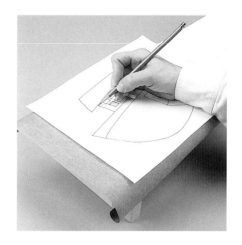

Lay carbon paper on facing, then position templates as desired and trace outlines. Referring to photo, paint animals and ark with small paintbrushes. When dry, paint eyes and mouths with black paint.

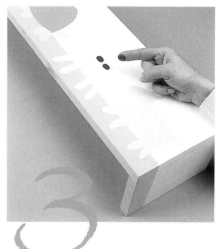

To finish, fingerpaint clouds with light blue paint and stripes, and polkadots on animals with black paint. Work slowly, being careful not to smudge paint. When dry, varnish entire cornice.

MATERIALS

Pre-assembled cornice *(Ch. 1)*
Tracing paper
Sponge brush
Assorted acrylic paint

Carbon paper
Paintbrushes: fine & pointed-tip
Clear, non-yellowing varnish

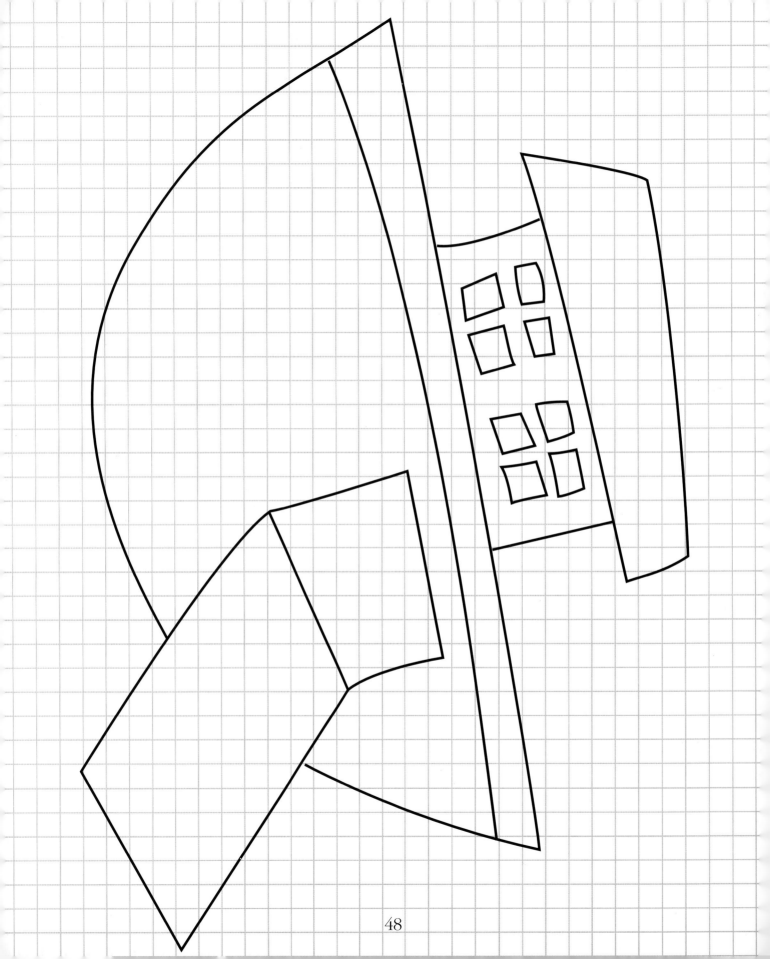

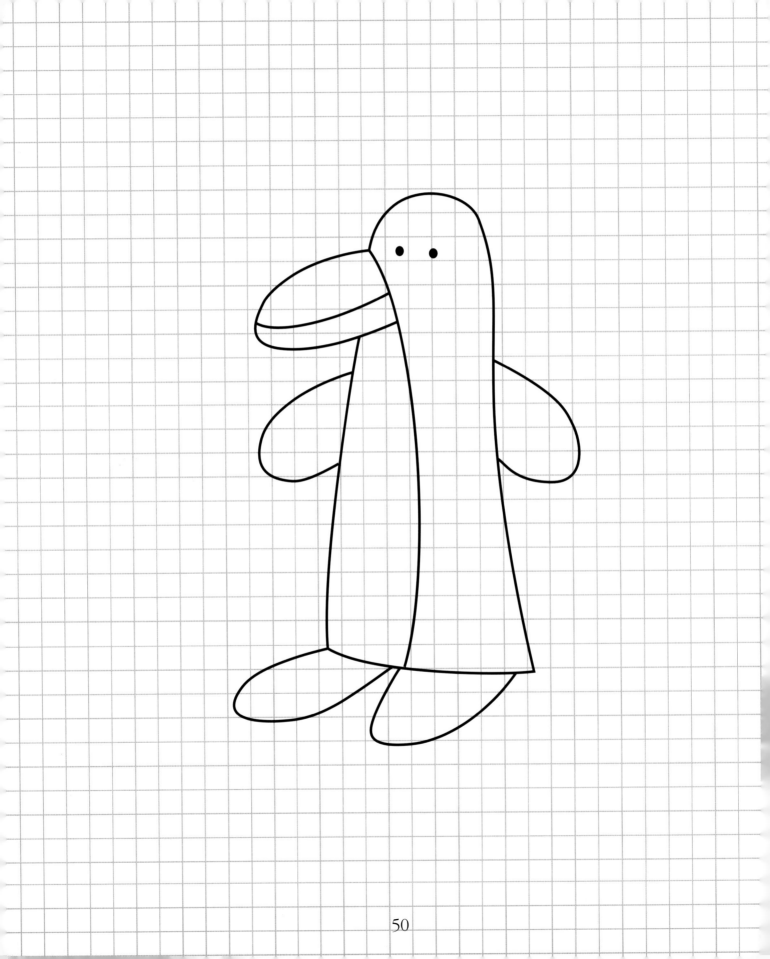

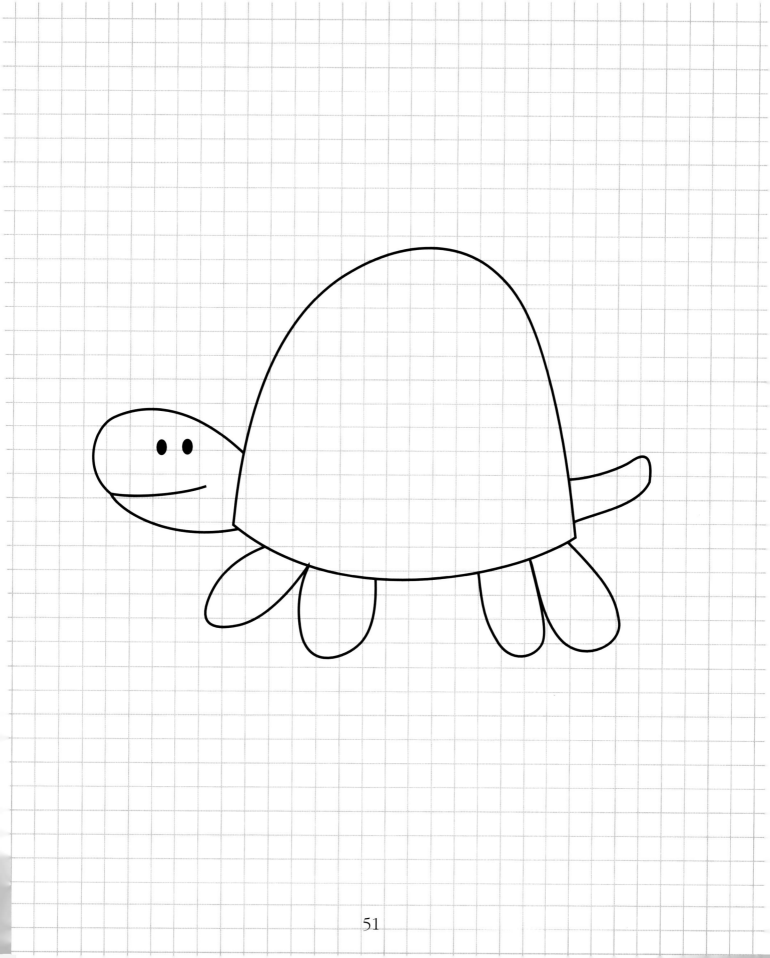

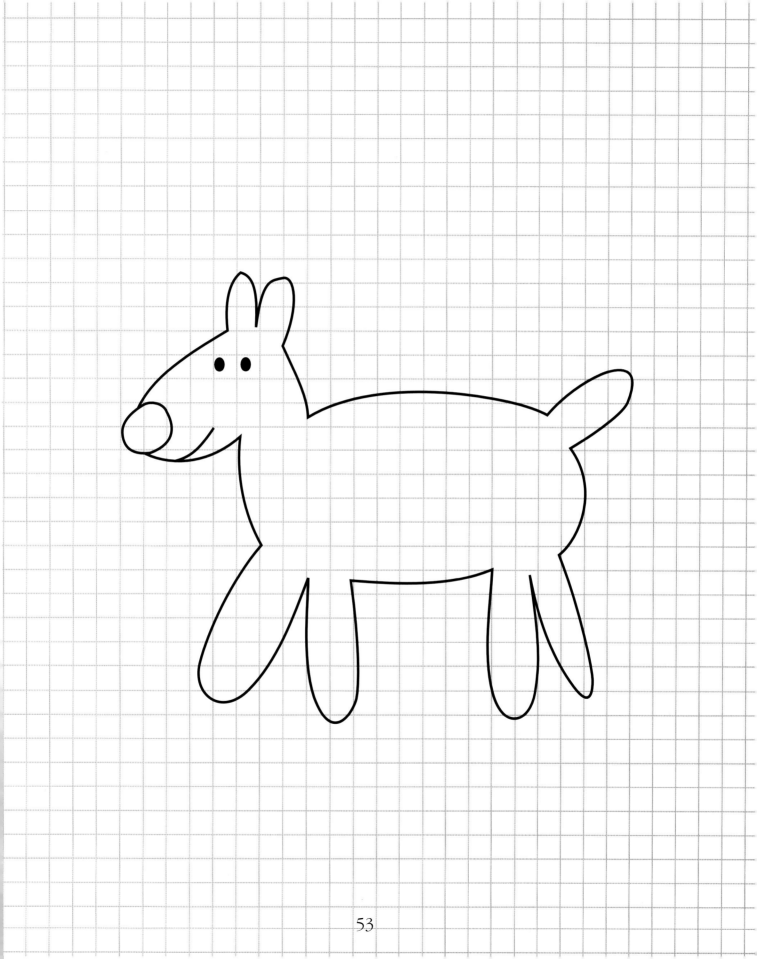

Child's Room
Choo-Choo Train

All aboard for some frolicking fun! This delightful choo choo is not only simple to make, but it can be crafted in less than an hour. Just cut scraps of fun foam into circles, squares, and other geometric shapes, then layer them across the cornice to create colorful train cars.

Enlarge templates to fit across facing, creating a separate template for each shape. Transfer to tracing paper and cut out. Lay templates on fun foam, lightly trace with pencil, and cut out.

Paint cornice with several coats of light blue paint; let dry. For track, paint 2" white stripe along cornice bottom. To add tracks, paint 1/2"-wide orange stripes diagonally over the white border.

Referring to photo, position shapes across facing, layering to create train cars. Add scraps of fun foam underneath top layers of foam to keep design level. Attach shapes to cornice with glue.

MATERIALS

Assorted acrylic paints
Pre-assembled cornice (Ch. 1)

Tracing paper
Fun foam

Pencil
Clear drying craft glue

1

2

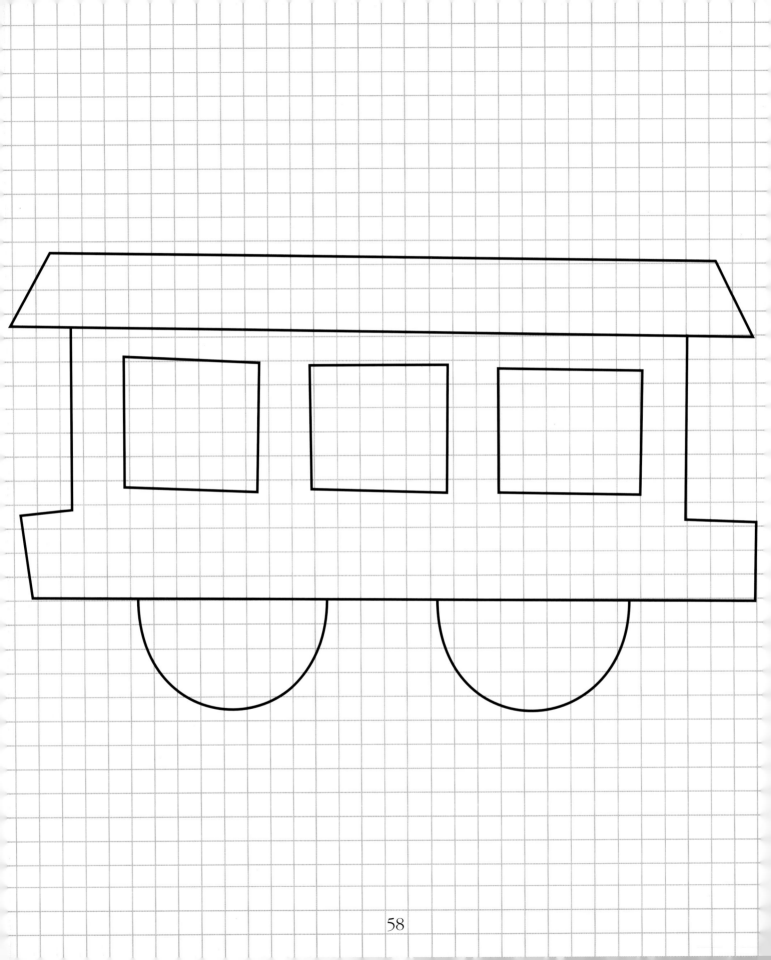

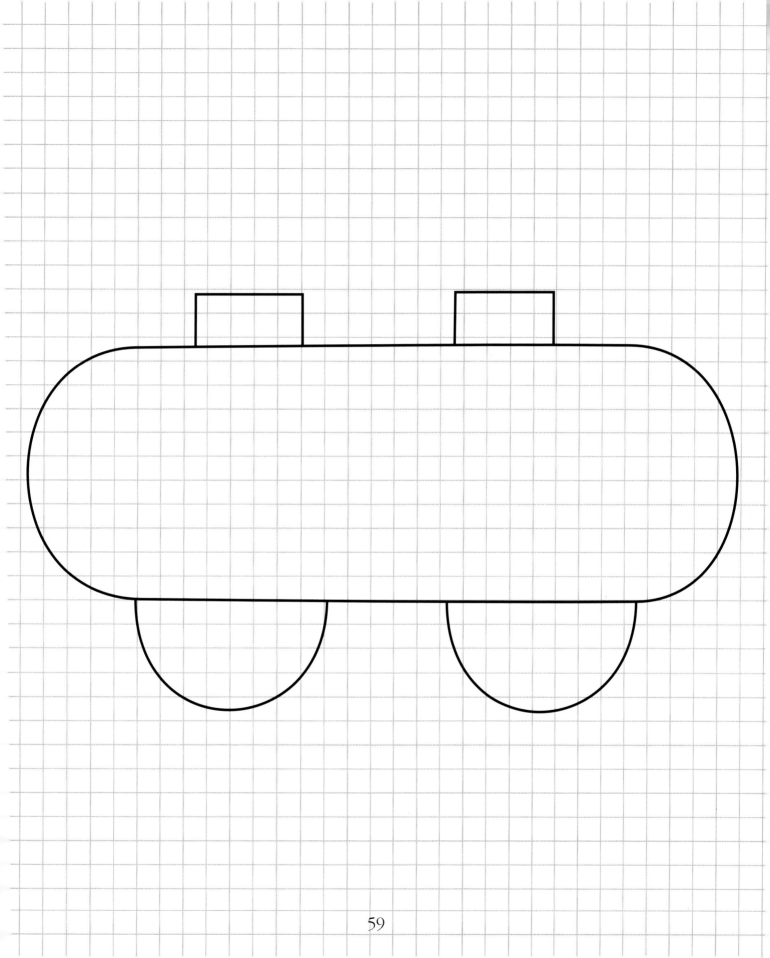

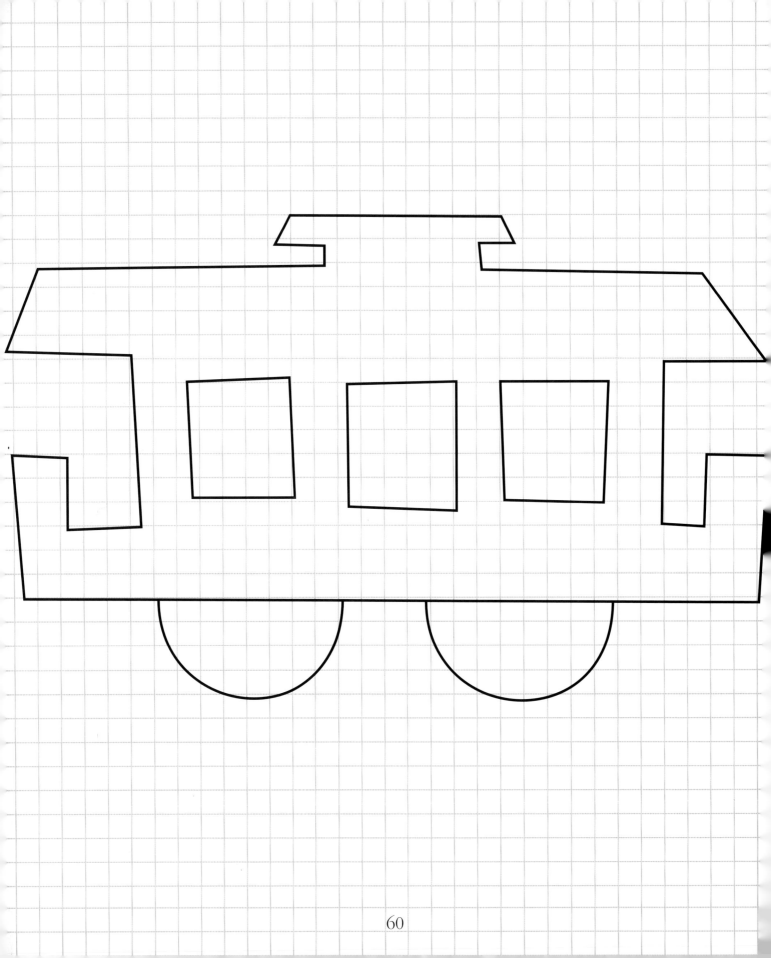

Fabulous Finds

*E*veryday objects have a surprizingly fresh look when used in creative and unusual ways. In this chapter, you'll discover projects crafted from household items that are inexpensive and easy to find. The results are delightful window treatments that do double duty as functional and decorative displays.

Den
Baseball Bliss

This sporty window treatment creates additional storage space for baseball equipment. Add to the effect by displaying trophies and ribbons on the window frame underneath.

2 Measure one-third down from top of window frame. Cut two pieces of rope twice length of measurement. Knot ends of each rope piece. Slip rope over center peg, then position bat in loop.

1 Paint peg racks with acrylic paint and let dry. Position one peg rack on each end of window frame top so that edge of rack is aligned with edge of window frame; screw in place with screwdriver.

3 Place baseballs in various lengths of netting; knot ends and hang from pegs. Referring to photo, hang baseball gloves and caps from pegs. To finish, position second bat on top of pegs.

MATERIALS

Acrylic paint & paintbrush

Two wooden peg racks

Screwdriver & screws

Rope

Two baseball bats

Baseballs

Netting

Baseball gloves

Baseball caps

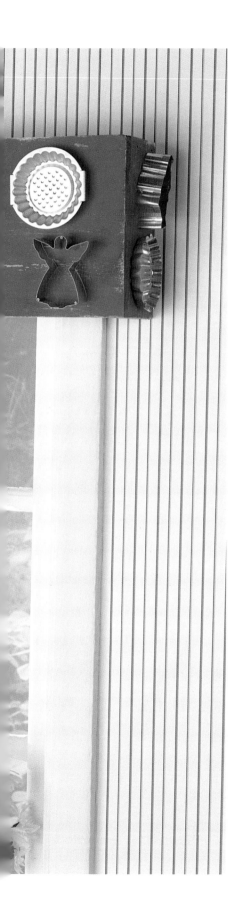

Kitchen
cookie cutter cornice

*Clean up kitchen drawer clutter by hanging cookie
cutters and miniature tart pans along the front
of a wooden cornice.*

1

Paint cornice with one color of
paint; let dry, then paint second
color on top of first. Continue
until all desired colors are used.
For distressed finish, sand to
reveal layers of paint underneath.

Position cookie cutters and tart
pans as desired on cornice front.
Using hammer and finishing nails,
secure cookie cutters by nailing
close to edges. Hot-glue tart pans
in place.

2

MATERIALS

Pre-assembled cornice (Ch. 1)	**Assorted tin tart pans**
Acrylic paints & paintbrush	**Hammer**
Sandpaper	**1½"-long finishing nails**
Assorted tin cookie cutters	**Hot-glue gun & glue sticks**

67

Den
Gone Fishing

*This crafty window treatment adds personality
to your decor, and it is a great way to showcase prized
fishing rods and a collection of sea shells.*

Position fishing rod diagonally so tip end falls at top center of window frame and reel is at one side. Position bracket to support reel, then screw in place. Repeat to place rod and secure bracket on other side.

Mark placement for screw at top center of window frame. Screw in place halfway into wood. Position one rod on bracket and screw; wrap fishing line around screw to secure. Repeat for other rod.

Fold and drape fish net evenly over center screw. Using push pins, secure net to window frame at sides so bottom edges form a swag. Continue draping net over push pins to create valance.

To finish the look, drape strands of small shells around push pins and over center screw. Add more push pins if necessary to secure. Evenly scatter assorted sea shells in fish net.

MATERIALS

Two fishing poles

Two wooden curtain
   rod brackets

Fishing line

Screws & screwdriver

Colored fish net

Push pins

Strands of small shells

Assorted sea shells

Bedroom
Memory Photo Collage

A cornice collage is an unexpected way to display antique photographs. By using Velcro to mount the frames, you can change the photographs on a whim.

Cut scrap paper into small squares and number. Arrange photographs on cornice front, then remove and position a numbered square in its place. Number photograph to correspond with paper.

Working on flat surface, position frame back on piece of black construction paper. Trace around outline and cut out. Repeat until construction paper is cut to size for all frames.

Cut Velcro™ into small pieces. Place one side on back of frame and one side on cornice; press frame in place to secure. Repeat for all frames, adding more pieces of Velcro™ if needed.

MATERIALS

Wooden frames in assorted sizes

Black construction paper

Scraps of paper

Antique photographs

Pre-assembled cornice *(Ch. 1)*

Velcro™ strips with adhesive backs

Kitchen
Spooling Around

*Capitalize on the curved form and natural finish of wooden spools
by arranging them in architecturally inspired designs.*

2

Draw small arc in center bottom of cornice and cut out with coping saw. Arrange spools on cornice front as desired, then glue in place with wood glue. When dry, add spools to cornice sides.

1

Position spool on top of scrap piece of wood. Place chisel across center, parallel to wood grain. Hammer chisel gently to split spool. Repeat to split all remaining spools in half.

3

To finish cornice, apply several coats of stain over spools and cornice board until desired color is achieved. Let dry between each coat. Seal stain with clear, non-yellowing varnish.

MATERIALS

**⅞"- diameter wooden spools
  (approximately 70)**
Scrap wood

1"- wide chisel & hammer
Pre-assembled cornice *(Ch. 1)*
Coping saw

Wood glue
Clear, non-yellowing varnish
Paintbrush & stain

CHAPTER 4

Quick-
Stitch
valances

*E*ye-catching valances have long been the proper topper for windows. Begin with a basic pattern, cutting and adapting it as needed to fit your window. When the stitching is complete, add stylish features to create a one-of-a-kind valance that reflects your personal style.

Bathroom
Cute as a Button

Nothing could be easier than embellishing a valance with pretty button patterns. Basic outlines and quilt blocks are among the simple shapes you can imitate.

Before glue is completely dry, stitch buttons to valance using buttonhole setting on sewing machine. Wipe buttons and needle after stitching each button so glue does not build up.

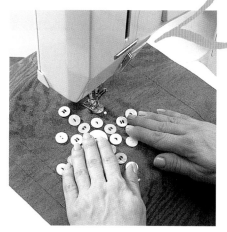

Lay finished valance on a flat surface. (Stitch a valance that is not too ruffled; otherwise the buttons will not show.) Draw geometric designs on fabric with pencil, arrange buttons, and glue in place.

MATERIALS

Simple ruffled valance (*Ch. 1*)

Dressmaker's pencil

Buttons in assorted sizes

Clear-drying glue stick

Sewing machine

Clean damp cloth

Living Room
Stenciled Autumn Leaves

A scattering of fall leaves adds seasonal flair to a ruffled valance. If you pair the valance with a cafe curtain, paint the leaves to match the curtain fabric.

1

Select leaf stencil of choice. Lay valance flat; position stencil on top. Mix one part textile medium with three parts acrylic paint. Dip stencil sponge into paint, dab on paper towel, then stencil leaf.

Continue stenciling assorted leaves randomly across valance front. For best results, use an almost dry sponge to stencil leaves. When dry, heat-set paint by pressing over valance back.

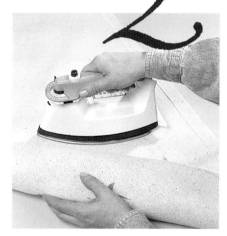

2

MATERIALS

Leaf stencil (Fall Leaves #3 from ReVisions®)

Standard ruffled valance *(Ch. 1)*

Transparent textile medium

Acrylic stencil paints in autumn colors

Stencil sponge

Paper towels

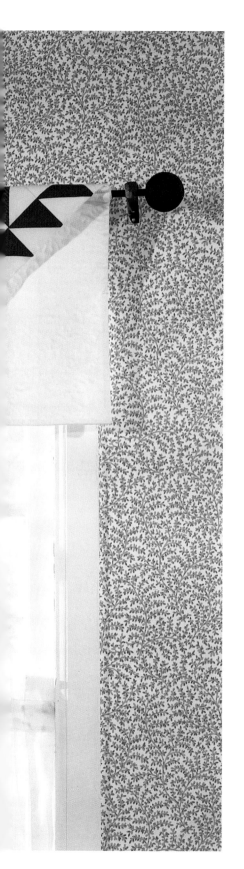

Bedroom
Bear Paw Quilt Topper

Add country charm to a window by draping a quilt topper over a basic flat valance. Sew the valance first, then stitch the pieced quilt topper to the top of the valance.

Position fabric and paper stack on sewing machine bed, then stitch along dotted lines on paper to make 2" squares for small blocks. Secure all threads at end of each stitching line.

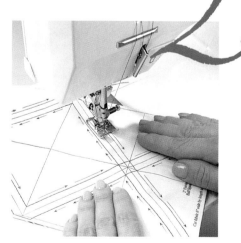

Install stiple-quilted valance on curtain rod. For quilt squares, stack fabrics right sides together on flat surface. Lay paper squares over fabric and pin in place; do not cut squares apart.

MATERIALS

Pre-stitched straight valance

White cotton & calico fabric

Printed paper (Triangles on a Roll) quilt for 2" squares

Pins

Sewing machine

Matching thread

Rotary cutter & plastic mat

Seam ripper (optional)

3

Remove pins, then lay fabric and paper stack on plastic mat. Using rotary cutter, cut out squares along solid lines. This creates both large and small triangle pieces from both fabrics.

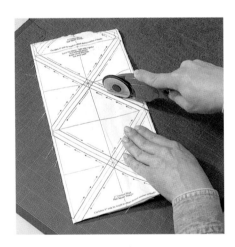

4

Carefully remove printed paper from all triangles. If needed, use seam ripper to gently coax paper away from seam line. Avoid trimming threads, if possible.

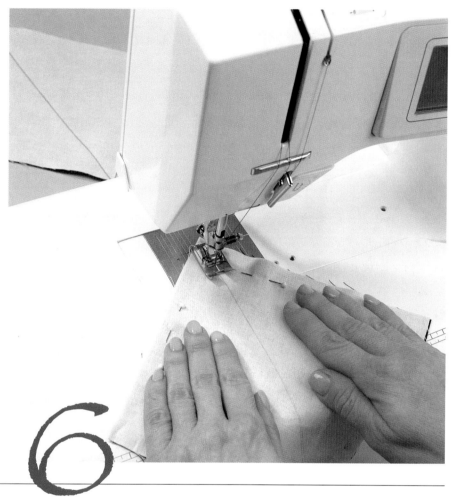

Open all seams and press flat. Referring to photo, position patchwork pieces on flat surface. Referring to window measurements, stitch as many pieces as needed to cover window.

Stack fabrics and paper again; stitch along dotted lines to create 6" squares. Referring to photo, piece triangles together to create pattern; stitch pieced squares together to form quilt topper.

Living Room
Sophisticated Scallops

*The decorative scalloped border on this traditional
valance is made by cutting around the flowers along the bottom and then
finishing the edge with satin stitching.*

Cut 5" width of fusible webbing the same length as valance. Position under bottom edge of valance and iron in place to stabilize fabric. Trim webbing to edge of fabric.

2

1

Stitch a standard valance with header; do not finish the bottom edge. Lay valance on flat surface. To determine placement for scallops, measure and mark chalk line along valance bottom, 3" from unfinished edge.

MATERIALS

Standard ruffled valance *(Ch. 1)*

Dressmaker's pencil or chalk

Ruler

Fusible webbing

Sewing machine

Matching thread

Embroidery scissors (optional)

3

Set sewing machine to 2mm satin stitch. With matching thread, begin stitching around outlines of flowers below chalk line. If needed, deviate from floral pattern so scallops are even in size.

When entire border has been satin-stitched, trim away fabric as close as possible to outside stitching line. If needed, use small embroidery scissors for hard-to-reach areas.

4

Once all fabric has been trimmed away, use 3-4mm stitch and satin-stitch over first stitching line. This ensures all loose threads and raw edges have been secured.

5

Bedroom
French Provincial valance

Wide, pressed pleats lend formality to this French provincial window treatment. For a professional finish, align the pleats from the center of the cornice board.

For piping yardage, measure length of cornice, multiply by two, then add 8" for seams. Referring to Chapter 1, cover cording with fabric to make decorative piping. Cut piping in half.

MATERIALS

Pre-assembled cornice *(Ch. 1)*

¼"- diameter cording

Contrasting fabric for piping

Quilt batting

Staple gun & staples

Two coordinating fabrics for cornice

Sewing machine

89

Cut two layers of batting same width as cornice plus 3", and same length as cornice front and sides plus 3". Wrap batting around edges of cornice, then staple in place along back.

2

3

To cover cornice, lay fabric flat, then measure and cut fabric same width as cornice and same length as cornice front and sides plus 3". Add ½" seam allowance to each long edge.

With right sides facing and raw edges aligned, pin and stitch each piece of piping to long sides of cornice fabric. Trim seams and press so piping falls along outside edges of fabric.

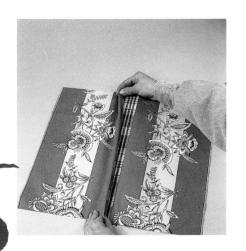

From same fabric, cut strips to fit across front and sides of cornice; add 4" for seam allowance. Cut fabric for pleats same length as strips. Stitch alternate fabric strips together. Press and pleat.

Hem pleats and press. Staple pleats evenly along bottom front edge of cornice board, then staple cornice fabric over batting so that piping is aligned with edges of cornice.

Den
All Tied Up

Looking for a clever way to make use of your husband's forgotten stash of neckties? With a few simple knots and a backdrop of rich velvet, create a colorful, modern treatment for your windows.

Cut velvet using window width and desired drop as guide. Drape velvet, bunching for fullness. Wrap elastic band around velvet, even with rod; tuck ends under and into bands to create pouf.

Wrap end of one tie over rod; knot as desired to secure. Continue wrapping and knotting ties, using different kinds of knots for each tie. Slide ties together to form three distinct groups.

MATERIALS

Assortment of dress ties

Decorative iron curtain rod

Velvet fabric

simple shutters

Because of their clean, classic lines, traditional shutters can be easily incorporated into any decorating scheme. Once you have made a sturdy, wooden shutter frame, you can embellish it with sewing notions, natural materials, and decorative papers that reflect your personal style.

Child's Room
Decorative Decoupage

*Make the most of wallpaper scraps and favorite
giftwrap by decoupaging the cutout designs
to the front of a painted shutter.*

1

Paint shutter frame and let dry. Close louvers. Paint one side and let dry, then open louvers and paint other side. If needed, apply masking tape around frame to avoid painting edges of shutter.

2

Cut out decoupage designs from from decorative papers. Choose designs that reflect the decorating style of the room and that are small enough to fit across sides and edges of the shutter.

Position designs as desired on top of shutter, overlapping if needed. Using paintbrush, apply decoupage medium to back of designs, then press firmly to wood. Smooth out bubbles.

3

4

When all designs have been applied to shutter front, brush a light coat of decoupage medium over top of designs to secure. When dry, apply varnish to all sides and louvers of shutter.

MATERIALS

Acrylic paints & paintbrush
Wooden louvre shutters

Painter's masking tape
Scraps of giftwrap & decorative papers

Decoupage medium & small paintbrush
Clear, non-yellowing varnish

Bedroom
No-Sew Quilt Squares

Cutting and fusing are the only skills needed to turn colorful calico squares into interesting geometric shapes. When the squares are "pieced" together, the finished shutters will have the look of country patchwork.

Divide shutter into equal-sized squares, then cut squares from foam core. Using a damp pressing cloth, stack and fuse three layers of fleece to one side of each foam core square.

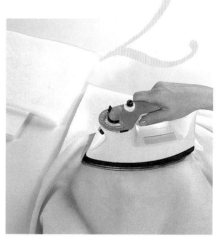

Paint stretcher strips with two coats of paint; let dry. Measure and cut poster board same size as shutter. Using staple gun, staple poster board around all edges of shutter front.

MATERIALS

Acrylic paints & paintbrush

Pre-assembled artist's stretcher strips *(Ch. 1)*

Poster board & foam core board

Staple gun & staples

Damp pressing cloth

Fusible fleece & webbing

Assorted cotton fabrics

Hot-glue gun & glue sticks

3

Cut fabric squares ½" larger than foam core squares. Cut medium squares 1" smaller and center squares 2" smaller from alternating fabrics. Fuse webbing to wrong side of all squares.

Center large fabric squares over foam core; fold fabric edges to back and fuse in place. Referring to photo, stack and fuse smaller squares on foam core square to form patchwork design.

Position squares on top of shutter so fabrics alternate and form patchwork pattern. Apply hot glue to edges of squares and press in place. Center and attach knobs along inside edge of shutters.

Living Room
Wallpaper Panache

A twist on tradition, these stylish shutters are made with heavy, embossed wallpaper called anaglypta. The wallpaper center provides ample privacy while the ribbon-laced borders allow light to fill the room.

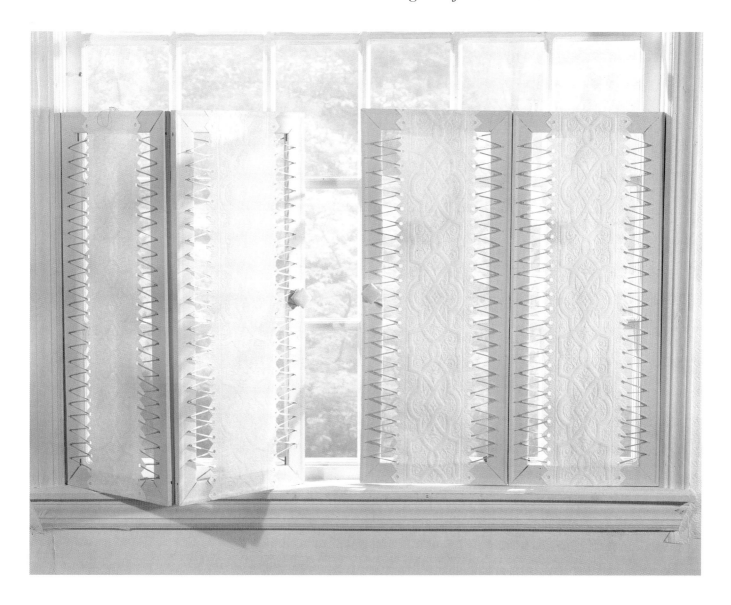

Using hole punch, punch hole in center of each point along both long sides of wallpaper. Avoid bending points of zigzag border and keep hands clean to prevent soiling front of wallpaper.

Paint assembled stretcher strips with two coats of paint; let dry. Cut two wallpaper pieces same length as shutters, plus 5". With points evenly spaced, cut 1"-wide zigzags along sides of wallpaper.

MATERIALS

Acrylic paints & paintbrush

Pre-assembled artist's stretcher strips *(Ch. 1)*

Scraps of anaglypta wallpaper

Hole punch

Clear drying craft glue

Hammer & ⅝" escutcheon nails

Clear tape

⅛"-wide silk ribbon or cording

Center wallpaper strip between sides of shutter. Apply glue along edge of wrong side of wallpaper, then fold wallpaper end under to back of shutter. Repeat for other end, pulling wallpaper taut.

Hammer nails along shutter sides, ½" from inside edge so each nail lies parallel to each punched hole. Make sure nails are securely fastened into wood and keep nails at same height.

Tape end of ribbon to wrong side of shutter to secure. Lace ribbon through punched holes in wallpaper and around nails along shutter sides. Cut and secure ribbon with tape at end.

Living Room
Woven Ribbons

Nothing could be easier than weaving ribbons to create a romantic window shutter. For a light and airy effect, leave narrow gaps between the edges of the ribbons.

1

Sand assembled stretcher strips smooth and wipe with damp cloth. Using paintbrush, paint all sides of stretcher strips and let dry. If needed, apply additional coats to cover woodgrain.

MATERIALS

Sandpaper & damp cloth

Pre-assembled artist's stretcher strips *(Ch. 1)*

Acrylic paints & paintbrush

Ribbons in assorted widths & styles

Staple gun & staples

Clear drying craft glue

Decorative knob

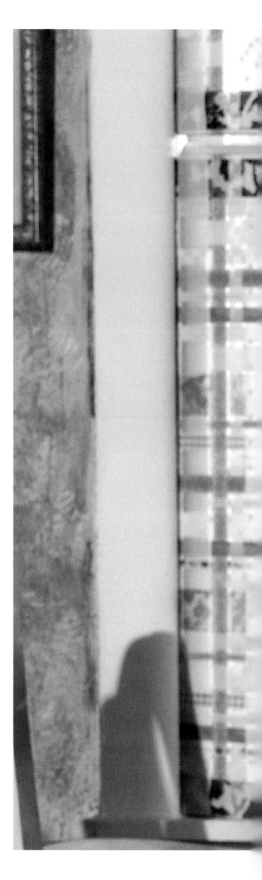

Fold end of one ribbon over short edge of frame and staple to back. Pull ribbon straight and taut to opposite end; fold end to back and staple in place. Continue to secure all lengthwise ribbons.

2

3

Working at top of one long side, fold and staple one ribbon end to back of frame. Weave ribbon through lengthwise ribbons, pulling taut, then staple end to back on opposite side of frame.

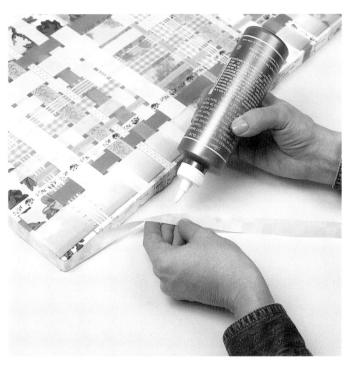

Continue weaving and securing
widthwise ribbons to cover frame.
To hide staples, glue piece of
ribbon around the outside edge
of the frame. Overlap ends and
hold in place until glue sets.

When glue is dry, reposition
ribbons, if needed, so space
between each is even. Measure
and mark placement for knobs at
center of shutters, 1" from edge,
then attach to shutters.

Den
Rustic Twigs

Bring a bit of the outdoors inside by covering a shutter frame with twigs. Leave the twigs natural for a masculine lodge look or whitewash them for true cottage style.

1

Measure inside of window frame. Cut two lattice strips the same length, and two strips half the width, minus 2¾". Position strips in place and assemble at joints with wood fasteners.

MATERIALS

¼" x 1⅜" lattice strips

Corrugated wood fasteners

Hammer

Sandpaper & damp cloth

Wood stain & paintbrush

Straight twigs

Pruning shears

Wood glue

Sand frame smooth then wipe with a damp cloth. Working on protected surface, apply stain on all sides of frame with paintbrush. Let dry, then repeat until frame is same color as twigs.

Beginning at one corner, position a twig diagonal to outside edges of frame. Using pruning shears, trim end of each twig diagonally so ends are cut parallel to edges of frame.

Apply wood glue along one side of cut twig and glue in place. Continue cutting twigs to size and gluing them to frame. Keep twigs close together for more privacy; farther apart for more light.

To make knob, cut four 2"-long twigs. Glue two twigs together along sides; repeat for remaining twigs. When dry, stack one set of twigs on top of the other and glue in place. Glue knob to shutter.

CHAPTER 6

Accents
of Interest

The whimsical and unique projects showcased in this chapter prove that window treatments are not always ordinary and conventional. In fact, the window is a perfect place to spotlight favorite photographs, treasures plucked from your garden, or time-honored crafts, such as decoupage.

Kitchen
Pretty Picket Fence

Based on the same pattern as a standard cornice board, this picket fence will add a garden accent to your kitchen. Weave silk vines around the pickets to complete the design.

Cut lattice strips into 10" lengths. Using miter box, cut one end of each strip at 45-degree angle; repeat for other side to form a point. Sand sides and edges of all lattice strips smooth.

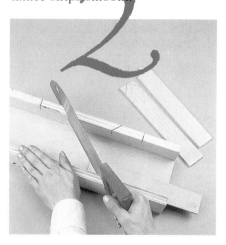

For cornice frame, cut three pieces of wood same width as window, plus 1½". Cut two pieces 3½" wide and four pieces 3" wide. Refer to photo above to nail frame together.

MATERIALS

1"x 2" pieces of wood

Coping saw & miter box

2"- long finishing nails

¼"x 1⅜" lattice strips

Sandpaper

Wood glue

White acrylic paint & paint
    brush

Strands of silk ivy

3

Evenly space pickets on cornice front so that bottom edges are 1" below cornice frame and all points are facing up. Glue pickets to cornice frame and let dry. Repeat for sides.

Using paintbrush, paint cornice with several coats of white paint. Let dry between each coat. Be sure to paint all sides of cornice frame, tops of points, and small bottom edges of pickets.

4

Mount cornice board at top of window. Weave silk ivy through pickets, draping as needed to form a swag effect. Secure ends of ivy by wrapping them several times around pickets.

5

Child's Room
Picture Window

If a picture is worth a thousand words, then this photo montage is sure to be a conversation starter. To tie the look together, select a theme, such as summertime, and then choose pictures that reflect the theme.

1

Remove glass and back from all frames. Measure and mark even placement for wood staples on back of top side of frame; hammer staples halfway into wood to secure. Repeat for all frames.

MATERIALS

Wooden picture frames

Wood staples & hammer

Acrylic paints & paintbrush

Assorted wooden shapes

Hot-glue gun & glue sticks

Assorted buttons

Photographs

Decorative eye hooks

¼"-wide satin ribbon

Randomly position wooden shapes and buttons along sides of frames. Using hot-glue gun, glue shapes and buttons in place. If desired, stack or layer shapes for interest. Place photos in frames.

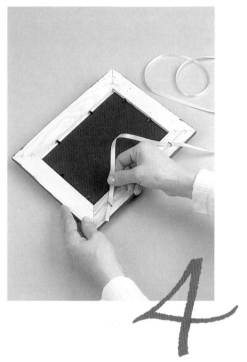

2

Choose contrasting colors for all frames, then paint all sides of frames with several coats of paint. Let dry. Paint wooden shapes in contrasting paint colors, let dry.

3

4

Mark placement on back for eye hooks along inside of window frame top; screw in place. Thread various ribbon lengths through eye hooks on window frame and staples on frame; knot ribbon and tie into bow.

Kitchen
Window Bouquets

Enjoy the bounty of your garden year-round with window bouquets of dried grasses, herbs, and flowers. For a crowning touch, drape the window frame with a raffia garland.

Gather one bunch of naturals and hold firmly. Wrap florist's wire around stems, about 3" below crown of bouquet. Continue wrapping several times to secure. Repeat to make all bouquets.

Lay dried materials into bunches of equal diameter. Mix dried materials for variety or create bunches from the same type of naturals. If needed, trim stems in bunches to even lengths.

Knot several pieces of raffia over florist's wire and trim ends. Place cup hooks evenly across window top. Hang bouquets from hooks with raffia. Finish by adding raffia garland across window top anchoring garland to decorate rod brackets. Trim ends.

MATERIALS

Dried grasses, flowers, & herbs	**Raffia**	**Small cup hooks**
Florist's wire	**Wire snips**	**Decorative curtain rod brackets**

Bedroom
Victorian Decoupage

The traditional art of decoupage becomes new and refreshing when used to decorate a valance. Use a simple curtain rod with a 2" return to mount the valance to the window.

1

Cut foam core same width as window and 10" deep. Using compass, divide bottom edge of foam core into four sections; draw equal-sized arcs for each section. Cut out with craft knife.

Cut Victorian images from paper. If necessary, use embroidery scissors to cut out hard-to-reach areas. Cut enough images to cover one-and-one-half the width of the valance front.

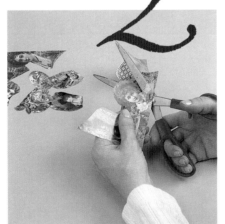

2

3

Following manufacturer's instructions, glue images to valance with Mod Podge, overlapping as needed. When dry, hot-glue cording around outside edges. Hot-glue valance to curtain rod.

MATERIALS

Foam core

Compass

Craft knife

Victorian decoupage papers or giftwraps

Embroidery scissors (optional)

Mod Podge decoupage medium

Hot-glue gun & glue sticks

$1/2$"- diameter cording

Den
Three-Dimensional Frames

Pretty as a picture, these frames take the art of pressed flowers to a higher level. By using dried leaves, twigs, and fruit slices, the finished pieces have three-dimensional qualities.

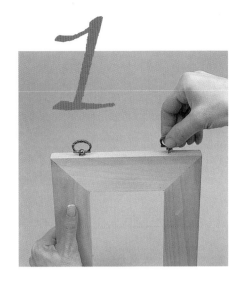

Remove glass and back from all frames. On top edge of picture frame, measure and mark placement for decorative eye hooks 1½" from side edges of frame; screw in place. Repeat for all three frames.

From construction paper, cut squares to fit inside frames, then cut squares from contrasting paper that are 1" smaller on all sides. Center and glue small squares to large squares.

Place paper inside frame and secure back. Arrange dried natural materials as desired along sides of frame and in center of construction paper. Glue in place with hot-glue gun.

Mark placement for eye hooks along top of window frame molding; screw in place. Thread several long pieces of raffia through eye hooks on frame and window; knot and tie into bow.

MATERIALS

Wooden picture frames for
   5" x 7" photographs
Decorative eye hooks

Construction paper
Clear drying craft glue
Dried fruit slices, cinnamon
   sticks, twigs, & leaves

Hot-glue gun & glue sticks
Raffia

INDEX

INDEX

INDEX